REBECCA N. CARMANT

SUNSHINE ON STORMY SEAS

Published by Lominy Books
Davie, Florida
www.lominybooks.som

First Edition, May 2015
Copyright ©2015 Lominy Books

The views expressed in this book are those of the author(s) and do not necessarily reflect those of the publisher.

All rights reserved. This book, or parts thereof, may not be reproduced in any form without permission. The scanning, uploading, and distribution of this book via the Internet or via any other means without the permission of the publisher is illegal and punishable by law.

Please purchase only authorized editions, and do not participate in or encourage piracy of copyrighted materials. Your support of the authors' rights is appreciated.

Cover images: Blue Skies/Martin Cathrae © 2010; Waves Crashing/Christopher Koppes © 2011; Butterfly/Schick © 2008; Hand/Shutterstock.

ISBN-13: 978-0-9910821-8-6

Printed in the United States of America

REBECCA N. CARMANT

SUNSHINE ON STORMY SEAS

"This collection of poems is like a warm hug in the strong arms of empowerment. The pieces are touching in Rebecca's pursuit and attainment of strength."

Mahalia Solages, author of *What Morning is This?*

"What a rush of emotions! Happiness. Fear. Outrage. Endearment. There is a word, a nudge—something for everybody!"

Martine Jolicoeur, blogger at *Me… Unfinished*

"A perfect combination of passion and talent. *Sunshine on Stormy Seas* took me home!"

Marylin Laurent, author of *Diary of an Innocent Dreamer*

TABLE OF CONTENTS

7	About the Author
9	Acknowledgements
13	You Don't Know Me at All
16	They Really Have No Idea
17	Know Who You Are
19	I Don't Want to Be
20	Too Young to Be Wise but Old Enough to Know
26	Who Cares?
27	Et la vie continue
31	J'ai le droit
33	Is It So Hard to Believe?
35	Je ne suis pas une allumette
36	So Sad Inside
37	Please Let Me Be
38	My Light
41	Good
43	The Inspiration to Write
46	Beautiful Words
47	Can My Pen Run Wild?
49	Bright Eyes
52	I Knew I Loved You
53	Sweet
55	I Want You to Live
58	Mon petit amour
60	Tout noir
63	Born Too Soon
65	Sometimes God Just Knows
67	The Lighter Side of Things
70	I Wish You Would
72	Long Overdue

75	Just Enough
77	Âme meurtrie
79	In Spite of It All
82	A Zest for Living
83	No Time
84	I Hate You
86	J'en ai marre
91	Bonheur de petite fille
92	Je n'oublierai jamais
96	Nostalgie
98	Bonjour, Soleil
100	Memories
103	La caméra
104	Regrets
105	Chéri, doudou, amour
108	Because I Love You and Miss You So
110	Thank You
112	You Have to Stay
114	What a Guy
116	The Story of Us
119	Regular Guy
121	Forty

REBECCA N. CARMANT
About the Author

It all started with a journal that Rebecca kept until her senior year in college. Words always fascinated her: She yearned for them, craved them, wrote them everywhere and, before she knew it, she was creating short stories, poems and essays. At 12, she had accumulated enough poems for a collection that she revisited often. She also composed lyrics that she belted out at home, too self-conscious to perform in public. She thought writing made her vulnerable because it exposed her inner thoughts. Her songwriting phase faded away, but not her burning need for self-expression. An avid reader of realistic fiction and philosophical thought, Rebecca had to find a way to reconcile her idealism to the realities of life, strengthening her interest in the human experience.

Born and raised in Haiti, Rebecca moved to the United States when she was 19. As a Haitian-American, she keeps her birthplace very close to her heart and memories of the land permeate her work. Rebecca advocates for many causes including autism, equity in education, cultural awareness, minority rights and social justice. She follows politics, has a flair for fashion, loves music and enjoys dancing. She cultivates a deep faith and spends her free time reading, gardening or relaxing with friends and family. She currently resides in South Florida with her husband and their son. She may no longer live in New York but she still thinks it's the coolest city! Her favorite sports teams are the New York Jets and the New York Yankees.

Rebecca holds a Masters degree in Education and is pursuing a doctoral degree in Leadership. She continues to pen her thoughts, giving voice to the battles she faces as a woman of color, a person of faith, and the mother of an autistic child.

ACKNOWLEDGEMENTS

To my husband Armand, my steadfast supporter,

I did it, honey! I finished the book! All these years, your love, your support, and your faith have been the wind beneath my wings. Thank you for being my sounding board, my mirror, my first audience. You've been a true partner throughout this writing adventure and I don't know how I would have made it this far without you. I love you.

To my son Cyril,

who inspires me to be a better person every day. I love you to pieces. Being your mom is my greatest joy.

This book is for the both of you.

I would like to thank M.J. Fievre who did double duty as my publisher and editor. Dear Jessica, thank you for telling me that I had a strong voice and taking me on as a new author. I couldn't have asked for a better editor or publisher to guide me through this process, catch my mistakes, and steer me in the right direction. Thank you for showing me the ropes and listening to my ideas. I am forever indebted to you.

To the amazingly talented Charlotte Howard, who captured my vision and recreated it with captivating dexterity. Thank you for working with me and taking the time to know me through my words. You nailed it. You really did.

I want to express my gratitude to Mahalia Solages, Marylin Laurent, and Martine Jolicoeur @MeUnfinished, for taking the time to discover my work and react to it. You've forged your own paths and I hope to follow into your footsteps.

This endeavor would have been impossible without the support of my family: my parents, grandparents, aunts, and uncles, who instilled in me, and later nurtured, my love of reading by providing quality books to an inquiring mind; this journey started with them. The books I read as a kid fanned my passion for words and my love of writing, so thank you for making it a rule to read whenever school was out; my siblings who indulge many of my whims but never hesitate to tell me the truth when I need to hear it; my cousins who never fail to support me and always know what to say to make me feel better. Your input made a difference and helped move this book along.

To the friends who've helped me every step of the way: What would I do without you? You've been after me for years to put my work out there. You've nudged, hinted, advised, and commented. I appreciate you and raise my glass to you.

I especially want to recognize: Myrna Laine-Hyppolite, Christine Cameau-Hyppolite, Elena Jean-François and Cassandre Thrasybule who were an integral part of this process and graciously agreed to let me bounce my ideas off them while I was writing the book. Thank you for taking time out of your busy lives to listen, to read, and to give me feedback whenever I asked.

I would be amiss if I did not mention the friends who've helped me develop my ideas for many of the pieces I wrote: Jennifer Fievre who pushes me to step out of my comfort zone, Katiana Pierre-Diaz who helps me navigate the emotional minefield, Joelle Damas whose willingness to embrace a new adventure inspires me to do the same, Barbara Faustin who listens to and helps me clarify my thoughts, and Gina Pierre-Louis who supported me from the early stages of this publishing journey.

To everyone who read my work and encouraged me to express myself over the years, thank you. Your opinion was instrumental in helping me hone my craft.

Without God and my faith in Him, none of this would have been possible. Writing is a blessing. Thank you, God, for giving it to me.

To my readers,

I hope this book creates a Pocket of Happiness in your life.

Yours,

R.C.

YOU DON'T KNOW ME AT ALL

You don't know me at all, you see.
You know just nothing about me.

You think you have me figured out
but, truth is, you don't know me at all.
Tell me what you know of my past,
of my present, of my future?
What do you know of what I think?
Of what I feel, of what I know?
What do you know of the layers
that make the *me* that you see here?
What do you know of my real life—
the one I keep from prying eyes?

You don't know me at all, you see.
You know just nothing about me.

You don't know when I come and go,
and if I do go anywhere,
the truth is: you never know where.
You don't know who my idol is,
if I have one, you don't know that.

You don't know what I like to do,
with whom I do the things I do,
or that I call myself Catholic
(Christian Catholic is preferred).

That I think of my heritage
as much as I do of my faith.

That being a woman matters
almost as much as being a mom.

You don't really know me, you see.
You really don't know me at all.

Do you know what makes my heart sing?
What scares the skin off of my back?
Do you know if I am afraid
to sleep alone, or if I'm not?
Do you know what provokes
the tears that I may shed?
Do you know that?

You know nothing of my regrets,
of my wishes, and of my dreams.
You know nothing of all the hopes
that I harvest within my heart.
Do you know why I get nervous
every time I hear certain words?
Why I keep some memories
safely tucked away in my head?
Do you know why I close my eyes,
breathe deeply, then pretend to smile?

You don't know me at all, you see.
You know just nothing about me.

Sometimes I wish that you and I could find
a way to bridge that gap, to overcome
whatever hurt still lingers there.
But you don't see me, you don't hear me.
Do you know how long I have tried
to get you to listen to me?

15// Sunshine on Stormy Seas

You don't know me at all, you see.
You know just nothing about me.

I guess it's just as well this way.
Too bad for you, just fine with me.

THEY REALLY HAVE NO IDEA

They really have no idea
just how much it matters
to know oneself, know who you are…

How much that does truly matter!

What happens when you don't really know:
Confusion, doubt, craziness.

You have to
try.

KNOW WHO YOU ARE

To find happiness, you turn away from who you are—as an individual, as a person. Under the false pretense of reinventing yourself, you masquerade as something you're not, something barely recognizable as the *you* you once were.

Oh, we all change and evolve, to really find ourselves, to become who we're really meant to be. We go through the motions on a road traveled by all, a road peppered with tears, poor judgment and bad decisions—embracing, rejecting, denying, confessing... asking questions, seeking answers, rebelling, accepting. Until we find the finished, found, accomplished self buried in the subconscious mind. *Our* self.

Running away from this self is not going to bring you happiness. It will not! Go ahead, ask others. They will tell you that happiness is to accept who you are: your past, your present, your heritage and race, your culture, the weight of your life experiences and chance encounters. Accept the impact of new relationships while preserving old ones. Accept that these relationships may widen your view of the world, but that they do not change the essence of who you are. Accept the way your mind absorbs knowledge and processes it to enrich your soul, the way it may strengthen your identity, but remember: What goes on around you should not change the real you—it should only enhance it.

If something speaks to you, strikes a chord deep within you, then it is the real *you* responding. Your strength resides in your sense of self—and no one can take that away from you. Your strength is not in the clothes you wear, the hairstyle you sport, or the music you like. Your strength is in knowing who you are. Your strength is a clear sense of these things that define you, these things that, in one million imperceptible ways, affect the way you relate to the world, the way you see yourself, think of yourself. And no matter how hard you try, you can't run away from it all.

God made you who you are and, whether you believe in Him or not, you are who you are. Born somewhere on this earth, part of a group that specifically grants you certain traits and attributes you can't deny. You may now hate who this person is but, sooner or later, you'll have to confront the face in the mirror.

Knowing who you are is a start.

Embracing who you are is the goal.

I DON'T WANT TO BE

I don't want to be a shark
I don't want to be a lion
I don't want to be an eagle
I don't want to be a fox.

Not a bear, not a tiger
Not a hawk or a spider
Not even an alligator.

I just want to be human.
Essentially, wonderfully,
amazingly human.

I want to be me: a person:
someone with dreams and desires.
I want to be me, whole and free
in my body, mind and soul.

I want to say yes to my truth,
embrace my own reality.

TOO YOUNG TO BE WISE BUT OLD ENOUGH TO KNOW

That life is not just
what you make of it
because it takes sudden,
unexpected turns.
(All you can do is
follow the curve
or risk losing your way.)

That instinct and love
are great companions
to your conscience.

That fear is paralyzing.
It can make you want
to crawl in a corner
and hide.

That feelings get hurt
many times over,
sometimes on purpose,
sometimes by accident.

That you know
you really love someone
when "he's the other part of me"
suddenly makes sense;
when you feel empty
because he's not here;

21// Sunshine on Stormy Seas

when your body grows cold
at the thought: "what if"

That what you choose to believe
will make you or break you
in times of great need.

That God really does exist
but He'll only come
when you call for Him.
(Have Faith!)

That it's good to pray
and to ask others to pray for you
so don't be afraid to tell others
what you are going through.

That, when you're desperate,
and don't know what to do,
you should start a prayer chain.
(It works!)

That having a great support system
comes in really handy
in difficult times.

That you should not forget
to thank those who stand with you.
Tell them how much
you appreciate them.

That you should not be afraid
to disagree
with the experts,

especially if you know someone
better than they do.
That people will say
what they want to say
and nothing you do
can change that.
(So true!)

That people you don't even know
will spread rumors about you.
(Ignore them.)

That knowing who you are
will go a long way
towards helping you
withstand adversity.

That you should confront life
on your own terms,
just as you've been living it.

That your best
will never be good enough
for some
(but do your best anyway).

That you should recognize
when you're wrong
and act accordingly.
Change your attitude
and learn from your mistakes.

That spoiling for a fight
wastes your energy

and accomplishes nothing.

That emotions run high
in times of crisis.
Watch your words:
you can't take them back
once they've been spoken.

That no one
really knows
everything.
Everyone
is looking for answers.

That there are facts
and then,
there are opinions.
Know the difference
between the two.

That your kids
will surprise you
in ways you never thought
they could.

That people change
as they grow, evolve and learn.
Accept that
or risk losing them.

That life is not fair
but that doesn't mean
that you should not be.

That a mother's love
spells devotion and sacrifice.
It is boundless, strong, powerful.

That friends and family
are the greatest gift.
They make the best allies.

That you should respect
those who matter
not just to you
but to your loved ones, too.

That while your world
is falling apart,
the earth keeps spinning
and people keep living.

That you should always remember
who you are
and what you believe in.
Don't let others define you.

That you should not let others
walk all over you.
Speak up.
Be heard.
Stand up for yourself.

That people will sense
your weakness
and go in for the kill.
(You better believe it!)

25// Sunshine on Stormy Seas

That kindness
will come to you
from the least expected sources.

That, as sure as the sky is blue,
the sun will shine again.

Let the love in your heart be your guide.
Let your faith be your wheel.
Let your conscience be your voice.

WHO CARES?

Who cares what you think,
what you do, where you go?
I know what I know;
the same goes for you.
Who cares what you say,
how you feel, how you look?
You want what you want,
and I want something, too.
Who cares that you're here,
waiting and hoping,
when you know quite well
that it won't change a thing?
Who cares about your passion
and the time you're wasting?
The clothes, the money,
all that you want to give?
I care about my life,
my choices, and my dreams.
My will is my own,
and my will has spoken.

ET LA VIE CONTINUE

On parle de moi
On parle de toi
On parle de nous
On parle de tout
Ainsi va la vie

Une main s'étend
puis se retrait
Une langue s'acharne
puis elle se tait
Et la vie continue

On se sent bien
On se sent mal
On a de la peine
On est heureux
Ainsi va la vie

Superficielle
Traditionnelle
Idéaliste
ou anarchiste
La vie continue

On cherche à plaire
ou à déplaire
On se sourit
ou on s'ignore
Ainsi va la vie

On fait la fête
avec un verre
On se réveille
en gueule de bois
Et la vie continue

On est mesquin
ou bien pantin
Fait montre de grâce
ou manque de classe
Ainsi va la vie

On veut parler
de tout ce qu'on sait
Va jusqu'à
inventer des faits
Et la vie continue

On subit
une déception
qui devient
une humiliation
Ainsi va la vie

Regarde en face
les ennemis
qui prétendent
être des amis
Et la vie continue

On froisse certains
sans le vouloir
d'un mot, d'un geste
sans trop savoir

29// Sunshine on Stormy Seas

Ainsi va la vie

On veut de toi
parce-que l'on croit
qu'on peut tirer
un sou de toi
Et la vie continue

On décide
d'enterrer la hache
On la reprend
dès qu'on se fâche
Ainsi va la vie

On commet
toutes sortes d'erreurs
On s'en rend compte
bien après l'heure
Et la vie continue

On est de droite
ou bien de gauche
Même l'indépendant
se doit d' choisir
Ainsi va la vie

On croit en Dieu
On n' croit en rien
On est seul maître
de son destin
Et la vie continue

On agit bien
On agit mal

Lucidité
ou bien folie
Ainsi va la vie

On ressent
toutes sortes d'émotions
qui font fi
de toutes conventions
Et la vie continue

Pour quelques uns
une vie de rêve
mais pour bien d'autres
un vrai cauchemar
Ainsi va la vie

A chacun
sa réalité
A chacun
sa propre vérité
Et la vie continue.

J'AI LE DROIT

J'ai le droit de vivre ma vie, à ma façon,
comme je l'entends.
Et pour cela prendre mon temps,
même si mon temps dure trop longtemps.
J'ai droit à mes opinions, à ma vision,
à mes espoirs, et à mes rêves,
et à mes propres raisons pour mes actions.
J'ai droit à toutes mes expériences,
qu'elles soient à tort ou à raison.

J'ai le droit d'avoir mes problèmes
et de chercher une solution.
J'ai le droit d'être qui je suis,
imparfaite, tout à fait humaine.
J'ai le droit de tendre la main
et d'aider ceux qui le veulent bien.
Et j'ai le droit de décider
s'il vient le temps de changer de ton.

J'ai le droit de tolérer
ce que les autres ne comprennent pas.
J'ai le droit d'adorer mon Dieu,
le droit à ma propre religion.
J'ai le droit de dire que je crois
en un seul Dieu, si c'est le cas.
J'ai le droit de vouloir l'aimer
sans être accusée de fausseté.
Et j'ai le droit de changer d'avis,
de reculer, de m'écarter.

J'ai le droit de m'assurer
sécurité, un peu de gaieté.
J'ai le droit de décider
de ne rien dire ou de parler.
J'ai le droit de protéger
ce qui m'est cher, de le garder.
J'ai le droit de dire oui
ou de dire non,
d'agir en toute honnêteté.

J'ai le droit de raconter
les moments qui m'ont fait pleurer.
J'ai le droit d'élever la voix.
J'ai le droit de m'exprimer,
à ma façon, n'importe comment.
J'ai le droit de m'énerver,
de me calmer, de m'excuser.
J'ai le droit de réagir
comme je juge bon pour le moment.

J'ai le droit de partager
les plus beaux moments de ma vie.
J'ai le droit de travailler
pour mon bonheur et mon bien-être.
J'ai le droit de reconnaitre
que je suis loin d'être parfaite.
J'ai le droit de refuser
d'être définie par des préceptes.
J'ai droit à ma liberté,
une liberté que je chéris.

IS IT SO HARD TO BELIEVE?

Is it so hard to believe
that we 're all created equal,
that, despite our differences,
we're all part of the human race?
Is it so hard to believe
that we all deserve happiness,
demand fairness, need dignity?
Is it so hard to believe
that we're meant to share Earth's bounty,
not meant to scare, not meant to tear?
Is it so hard to believe
that we should respect each other,
not yell or shout, not point fingers?
Is it so hard to believe
that all lives matter,
that all lives count
regardless of race, of color?
Is it so hard to believe
that we all have
the need to love,
the need to breathe,
the need to live?
Is it so hard to believe
That beneath our differences
lie many deep influences?
Is it so hard to believe
that we all feel the same feelings,
cry the same tears,
smile the same smile?
Is it so hard to believe
that we all use our voice to speak,

our head to think
our hands to touch?
Is it so hard to believe
that we're all created equal,
that, despite our differences,
we're all part of the human race?

We're all part of the human race.

JE NE SUIS PAS UNE ALLUMETTE

Je ne suis pas une allumette
rangée dans une boîte
qui prend feu simplement
au bon gré de son maître.
Je suis un brin de paille,
emporté par le vent,
qui s'enflamme plutôt
au gré de la chaleur

différents cercles
différentes opinions
      Je m'aventure
          un peu partout
avec mes convictions—
opinions personnelles
Et si je m'échauffe
 c'est parce-que je le veux,
      non parce qu'un autre
          me pousse à le faire.
Parfois il faut parler
Parfois il faut agir

pour que les choses changent.

SO SAD INSIDE

Why do I feel so strange in my skin?
Why do I feel like I don't belong?
Why am I here and not back home?

Why these cutting looks when I play my music?
Why all these rules and regulations?

Why do they frown when I arrive?
Why do they smile when they want to bite?
Why do they want me to act like them?
Why do they want me to be someone else?

Why be here if I can't be happy?

Why can't they accept me for who I am?
Why do I feel like they've condemned me?
Why do I feel so sad inside?

PLEASE LET ME BE

Please let me
do what I really want to do,
feel what I really want to feel,
say what I really want to say.
I don't want to be in the box anymore.
I want to feel free, free, free!
I want to take flight
from the top of a mountain
and get a bird's view
of the world around me.
I want to feel the thrill
that others are feeling.
I'm sitting in this chair
watching life pass me by,
but I want to be *me* now.
If you please, will you let me go?

MY LIGHT

Music.
Music is my light.
The tempo, the vibe, the rhythm, the sounds.
Happiness. Giddiness. Sadness.
Takes me back in time.
Brings me back to now.
Music is my light.

Singing.
Singing is my light.
The melody, the words, the message, the joy.
Happy songs. Sad songs. Songs that move me.
Singing is my light.

Dancing.
Dancing is my light.
Twirling, turning. Moving hips.
Tapping feet, bobbing head, raising arms.
A beat through veins and bones.
Dancing is my light.

Talking.
Talking is my light.
Talking to family, to friends.
Joking, teasing, gently probing.
Pouring out words and sharing thoughts.
Exchanging ideas. Expressing feelings.
Talking is my light.

Reading.
Reading is my light.
An article, a book. A window into worlds unexplored.
An escape from troubles, from stress.
Reading for laughs, reading to dream,
reading to know so much more.
Reading is my light.

Haiti.
Haiti is my light—
cherished land of birth,
of sweet childhood dreams.
Land that saw me grow,
that taught me so much,
that defined, developed, polished
a strong sense of self, of identity.
Haiti is my light.

Writing.
Writing is my light.
Part of my soul-searching self.
A way to say what I cannot express.
A beacon, a whistle, a white flag of peace.
A shortcut to God's given grace.
Writing is my light.

Loving.
Loving is my light.
Loving my husband. Loving my son.
My family, my friends.
Loving that I'm alive.
Finding delight in life's sweet surprises.
Loving is my light.

Praying.
Praying is my light.
An acceptance of things I cannot understand.
A testament of faith, of gratitude, of hope.
Praying is my life vest in life's troubled waters.
Praying is God's hand on my too frail shoulders.
Praying is my light.

God.
God is my light.
His Grace has allowed me to find the light within.
Music is a gift He's given me freely.
The dancing, the talking, the singing and praying:
God has given me ways to shine my light through.
God is my light. God is my light.

GOOD

A "good person" is ridiculed,
scorned, almost ostracized.
Others assume a "good person"
couldn't possibly "get"
their "real problems."
A "good person"
is almost like a plague:
something from a world
that no longer exists.
There was a time when "good" was in,
but "good" is now "passé." Overrated.

A good person comes with a set
of non-expectations (they think):
She doesn't fight for her rights (they say).
She doesn't question.
A good person *always*
does the right thing
and *always*
lets things go because
"really, you know better than that"
(they often tell her)
and, you know,
"you are so much better than that."
So it's not that others
don't respect "good people."
They do. From afar.
What's not to respect?
Good people have a heart, listen
to their conscience, and generally

do the right thing.

But *precisely* that's what
makes them boring.
It's like everything else
in this world.
What's not shocking, nasty, violent,
is not exciting, is it?
Good people? Ah!
There's nothing to see here.
What a waste of time.
"Suckers!" they say
when good people
fall for their old tricks.
"That would never happen to me."

I hear,
"You won't get far by being nice."
But good people are not stepping mats.
They don't actually let everyone
walk all over them.
They do stand up to others
when they have to,
if they need to.
They're just not always
"witches" or "jerks."

How about falling
somewhere in the middle?
Neither good or bad?
Is this good enough for this world?

THE INSPIRATION TO WRITE

Writing comes
from a thought, an image,
an idea, a vision,
from an experience, a song,
a picture, a touch,
from an illusion, a fact,
from victory or defeat.

Writing comes
from words uttered by strangers,
from words spoken at home,
from words read in a book,
a story remembered.

Writing can start
with hello or goodbye at the door,
with an embrace, a handshake,
a kiss or a hug,
with a smile—watery, shaky, brilliant
with a tear—lonely, tremulous, slow.

It can start with a fight,
words spoken in haste.
It can come
with anger—deep, strong and true.

Writing can come from
nature's indelible beauty,

from the sight of the sea—
so blue and so vast,
eternally ebbing and flowing along,
from the soothing sounds of waves
crashing gently on the shore,
from the whistling of wind
rustling through leaves on a tree,
from the colorful new wings
of a brand-new butterfly.

The urge to write may come
after a walk in the park,
after looking at flowers,
after going for a swim.

Writing may very well come
from the birth of a baby,
from special accomplishments,
milestones and celebrations,
from birthdays, weddings, graduations,
christenings, and first communions.

Writing may come
from divorce, loss, and abuse,
a sincere expression of pain,
an echo of secrets held deep within.

Writing can voice strong beliefs,
faith and principles.
It can shape the dreams
of a future yet unknown.
Expose the truth, emphasize facts.

It can be inspired
by love—magical and strong,
by sadness, by joy,
disappointment, and deceit,
by pride or surprise,
boredom or fright.

Writing comes from within us
from around us, from our world.
Writing mirrors what living
is really all about.

BEAUTIFUL WORDS

I wish I could turn beautiful words into
tiny, colorful butterflies that would fly away
on the wings of the wind
to land softly in the hearts of the scared and lonely.
I wish I could turn words into a symphony,
an orchestra of lullabies to soothe the soul,
ease the spirit,
of those who need to hear
whispers of love, of peace, of friendship, and of hope.
I wish I could let words fly up, up to the sky,
up to the heavens, way up to God in His Kingdom.
Maybe send a special message, maybe for Him
to send one back.
I wish I could transform my words,
and let them become what they should be,
let them find their way to the ones
who are searching for just such words.
I wish I could turn all of my words
into beautiful gifts of love.

CAN MY PEN RUN WILD?

Can my pen run wild?
Can I let it? Should I?
Can I let the words dancing in my head
come alive on paper as if in a dream?
Can I go "blah-blah-blah," and "tra-la-la-la-la?"
Can I make laughter come alive with letters?
Can my smile take shape under those keys?
Can you see the feeling pushing me forward,
giving me wings and making me fly?
Can you understand how I want to write,
just write anything that comes to my mind?
Can you see the need to dance with my thoughts,
whatever they are, whatever they mean?
Can you feel the warmth of my love for life—
family and friends, can you see it shine?
Can you see how God is guiding me now,
spearheading my life and leading the way?
Can I share with you how I love to feel
the breath of sea air that brushes my face
ever so gently? How I love to walk
on freshly cut grass, and love to hear
bees buzzing around, and birds chirping
loud way up in the trees?
Summertime fever, summertime dreams,
let my imagination run wild, unbridled.
Let me just sound silly if I happen to be.
Whatever my mood, let it come out freely,
be it giddy or sad, excited, proud, or mad.
Let it all out, I say, Let it flow out of me.
Words are like good old friends.
They give shape to my thoughts,

open up the door to other dimensions.
They strengthen me, ground me, keep me in check.
Words are my best allies, my trusted confidents.
They are a part of me, hidden safely within.
They are what I keep to myself the most
to share with you
only when my pen runs wild.

BRIGHT EYES

Can't help feeling happy
when I look into your eyes
and see them shining bright
and see them full of life.

Can't help feeling happy
when I look into your eyes
and still see the infant
who lived in the NICU.

You had those same bright eyes:
Eyes that said, I'm alive
Eyes that said, I am here
Eyes that spoke without words
Eyes that made others care.

Those eyes were the reason,
so many fought for you—
your nurses, your doctors,
caretakers, and others:
they were all inspired
by your shiny bright eyes,
and, in turn, they unveiled
their deep humanity.

A nurse's kind heart
placed with careful hope
a prayer for healing
on Jerusalem's wall.

She, too, took care of you
and was touched by your eyes
as you lay so fragile
in your small NICU crib.

Another nurse told us that
your name was uttered
every night in prayer
at the dinner table.
She was touched by your eyes,
she told her family,
and so they prayed for you,
made you part of their home.

All this and so much more
because of your bright eyes.

Those bright eyes that followed
every move, every sound.
They watched me carefully
as I sang lullabies
or held you in my arms
for precious mommy time.

Those bright eyes opened wide
when your dad stood close by
and whispered, "Hi, Tonton,"
as he touched you gently.

We looked into those eyes
and could tell, could just feel
that you were real indeed,
that you had come to stay.

51// Sunshine on Stormy Seas

Those bright eyes followed us
Those bright us tracked our moves
Those bright eyes understood
more than we thought, I'm sure.
Those bright eyes stayed the same
as you followed your course
from NICU warrior to NICU graduate.

And now you are such a lively,
happy-go-lucky kid.
You live life so simply,
so fully, with such joy.
Bright eyes full of laughter,
in a fit of giggles.
Bright eyes with a twinkle
when you're up to mischief.

Looking into those eyes,
I know that I was right—
right not to let you go,
right to put up a fight,
right to demand more,
right to believe in you.

I hope you understand,
that you feel it somehow:
you are very much loved,
accepted and embraced.
You're very much valued
because you were wanted.
As you did in the past,
as you're doing today,
let those bright eyes of yours
speak their very own truth.

I KNEW I LOVED YOU

I knew I loved you from the moment I first found out.
Knew I would love you
whether you came out gray or blue.

I knew I loved you
as I carried you through the months.
Knew I would love you as I talked to you, sang to you.

I knew I loved you as I searched for the perfect tune.
Knew I would love you
as I played different beats and sounds.

I knew I loved you as they said you'd come too early.
Knew I would love you as I laid in that bed, waiting.

I knew I loved you as soon as I heard your first cry.
Knew I would love you as soon as I laid eyes on you.

And I did.

I marveled at all of your toes,
at your fingers and at your nose,
inspected the folds in your skin,
looked at your eyes, looked at your ears.

I knew I loved you right away,
with all my heart and all my soul.
Knew I would love you for always.

I will love you forever more.

SWEET

Sweet is when we cuddle
        while watching your favorite show.
Sweet is when you hold my hand
           even in front of your friends.
Sweet is when I get a card
              with funny pictures,
                    misspelled words.
Sweet is when you offer a smile
        because you're playing nice.
Sweet is when you hold my neck
           because you'd like a kiss.
Sweet is when you call for me
              and come crawling in my bed.
Sweet is when you start laughing
      just because *I* am laughing.
Sweet is when you shout with joy
          when I pick you up from school.
Sweet is when you feel so safe
            because we are together.
Sweet is when you try so hard
    to do what I ask you to.
Sweet is when you do your work
           even if you don't want to.
Sweet is when you ask for help
              when you can't do it alone.
Sweet is when you ask to do some things
       without any help.
Sweet is when we watch you sing
         on stage during school concerts.
Sweet is when we see you jump
            because you're so excited.

Sweet is when you show your work
        with pride brightening your face.
Sweet is when you share with me
          all of your favorite games.
Sweet is when you say to me,
            "Look at my pictures! Look, Mom!"
Sweet is when you let me know
       that you got in big trouble.
Sweet is when I watch you grow
         and become independent.
Sweet is when, on Sunday nights,
            we work on science projects.
Sweet is when I watch you read
       by yourself, with no one's help.
Sweet is when you get curious
         and come standing next to me.
Sweet is when you take my hand
            because you want me to dance.
Sweet is when you say the words
       that I always want to hear.
Sweet is when you hug me tight and say,
         "I love you, Mom."

I WANT YOU TO LIVE

You may not have had the most perfect birth
but, from the very start, you were a perfect match.
You may not be living "the most perfect life"
but you complete my life and make it perfect.
I want you to live.
If God did not want you to be here,
you would not be alive at this moment in time.
So I want to help you get over your fears
and maybe you'll help me get over mine, too.

I want you to live.
I want to prepare you for what lies ahead,
when you're all grown up and I'm no longer there.
I want you to live the best life you can
and so I fight all these little fights.
I fight for your right to an education,
your right to learn the best way you can.
I fight for your right to a normal childhood,
your right to be just another kid.
I ask and look around, try this and try that,
as I want you to live and rise to new heights.
I want you to see things and do things
and try things and learn things.
I want you to explore and go places.
I want to push you when you're being stubborn,
I want to whisper, "Keep going. Don't give up!"
Despite all my fears, despite not knowing
what the future holds
I want you to live.
I want to see you conquer challenges.

I want to celebrate your wins
and soothe away your hurts
as you live the life you were given,
the best way you know how, the best way you can.

So what if I have to hold your hand a little longer?
So what if I have to guide your steps a little more
and show you where the holes are
when you are on the road?
I will not allow others to define who you are,
to define what you are, what it is you can do,
to pretend to know you when they've never met you,
to make what they think are the best decisions
when they could not care less what kind of life you live.
Some of them feel you are more trouble
than you're worth
but I want you to live.
When no one knew for sure
what would become of you,
God wanted you to live.
When some who've worked with you
came close to giving up,
you surprised them all.
You deserve to live life
as it's meant to be lived.
You have the right to try,
to succeed or to fail,
the right to know joy and feel love,
however they may come,
whenever they may come.
Some may not understand
why I want you to live.
They might have no idea
why I even bother.

57// Sunshine on Stormy Seas

Well, now they will know:
that it's because I do
I really, really do
really do want you
to live your best life.

MON PETIT AMOUR

Mon petit amour, je t'ai
aimé avant même que tu ne sois né.
Dès que j'ai su que tu existais,
tu as eu une partie de mon cœur.
Je t'ai aimé au cours des jours
où tu étais dans un cocon.
Je t'ai aimé lorsque, trop tôt,
tu es arrivé dans ce monde.
Mon petit amour, tu ne comprends pas
ce que c'est que d'aimer comme ça.
Pour toi, ma foi s'est affermie,
m'a fait prier pour un miracle.
Mon petit amour, quand je t'ai vu,
j'étais heureuse de te connaître.
Je me suis assise à tes côtés
pour te regarder, t'admirer.
Je m'étonnais de constater, qu'en fait,
il ne te manquait rien.
Tu avais tes dix petits doigts,
tes dix orteils, et tes oreilles.
Je ne m'étais pas imaginée
que tu serais aussi parfait.
Mon petit amour,
je t'ai bercé avec ma voix toutes ces nuits.
Tu étais encore trop fragile
pour reposer entre mes bras.
Déjà, lorsque tu entendais ma voix,
tu essayais de regarder,
tournais la tête pour me chercher.
Je n'arrivais pas à y croire.

Tu connaissais déjà ta mère.

Mon petit amour, je me rends compte
que tu grandis, deviens plus fort.
Je suis heureuse d'être témoin
de tes progrès, de tes succès.
Mon petit amour,
je veux te voir continuer ainsi à grandir,
à confronter tous les obstacles,
à les conquérir peu à peu.
Mon petit amour, que Dieu te garde,
qu'Il te protège, te réconforte.
Le plus beau cadeau de ma vie,
 je l'ai eu lorsque tu es né.

TOUT NOIR

Ce soir-là, j'ai vu tout noir.
On m'a appelée pour me dire qu'il fallait venir.
Tout de suite.
Un véritable cauchemar.
Le trajet m'a paru très long. Autour de moi,
tout était noir, effrayant, agonisant.
Je n'arrivais pas à respirer, donc j'ai crié
pour ne pas étouffer.

Ce cauchemar, la peur et la colique qu'il a engendrées.
Cette nuit affreuse et douloureuse,
incroyablement cruelle.

Je n'arrivais pas à penser, ne savais que dire ni que faire.
Je me suis raccrochée à ma foi,
me suis rappelée mes prières.
J'avais le ventre noué en cordes,
un arc de feu autour des reins.
Je me tordais les mains et hurlais, impuissante,
en larmes, impatiente.

Je refusais de croire au pire.

Je demandais à Dieu dans ma peur,
de m'épargner cette douleur.
Ce que j'avais de si précieux,
que j'avais accueilli et accepté,
pouvait-Il vraiment me l'enlever?
Comme ça, sans mise en garde?
Je ne pouvais pas respirer…

J'ai vu tout noir sur le chemin;
j'ai vu tout noir auprès de ceux
qui essayaient de me préparer;
ceux qui me tenaient la main,
voulaient que je fasse mes adieux,
pour ensuite m'en aller.

J'ai vu tout noir, malgré les lampes
et le clignotement des moniteurs.
J'ai vu tout noir dans la chapelle,
où je croyais devenir folle.

Ce soir-là : incompréhensible, infernal,
insupportable, intolérable.

Un homme de Dieu est arrivé,
un pasteur habillé de noir.
Il s'est assis non loin de moi
mais je n'ai pas voulu lui parler.
Il m'a dit lui aussi que je devais me préparer,
m'attendre au pire et l'accepter.
Mais j'ai refusé d'écouter; je l'ai ignoré.

Qu'il m'agaçait!
S'il ne pouvait pas m'appuyer,
lui qui devait en savoir plus, alors,
au moins qu'il se taise!

J'ai vu tout noir quand en voiture,
on m'a dit qu'il fallait le suivre.
On le menait autre part pour une dernière tentative.

J'ai vu tout noir.
J'ai trébuché; ne savais plus ce que je disais.

Je me taisais et puis priais, me lamentais et puis pleurais.
J'ai vu tout noir dans une chapelle
(Il y en avait une à chaque fois!).

Je n'en pouvais plus, m'affaiblissais,
commençais à me résigner.
J'ai vu tout noir, agenouillée devant le tabernacle fermé,
mes yeux tournés vers une peinture:
Jésus entouré de médecins.
J'ai vu tout noir; n'en pouvais plus de demander,
de supplier.

Puis… une chose étrange s'est produite.

J'ai senti comme une lumière
qui scintillait dans le trou noir.
J'ai senti comme une main,
qui me soutenait, m'affermissait.

Une dame s'est jointe à moi,
a demandé ce qui n'allait pas.
Elle a intercédé, demandé à Dieu d'écouter…
Je ne sais pas ce qui s'est passé.
J'étais dans l'ombre, comme hébétée,
mon cœur tout à côté de moi.

Je voyais tout noir.
Mais de ce noir, j'ai entrevu une étincelle.
Je ne sais pas d'où elle est venue,
cette paix que j'ai ressentie.

Mais je ne pleurais plus; j'attendais.
Il ne faisait plus tout à fait noir.

BORN TOO SOON

We wanted you, you know.
We prayed and planned for you.
But twenty-four weeks:
just a little too soon.

We prepared and researched all we could.
We followed the roads traced in our youth,
fulfilled expectations and worked hard at it all.
We just did not expect that you would come so soon.
This was not the way things were supposed to go.

Marching today, your dad and I saw the signs:
too small and too fragile for this world.
You, too, were born like this. Too small. Too fragile.
And we were scared
And we wanted to predict
what your future would hold.

Had someone played a trick on us?
How could this have happened?
We got in for the ride and buckled our seatbelts
as the shock settled in, like a dark winter night
that left us cold and alone, disconnected and lost.
Disoriented: no longer on the map.

We were angry with God for a while I recall.
We did not understand why He sent you so soon.
Yet, he kept you alive
through those rough days and nights.

For months, the NICU was our home.
Many people met you
and fell in love with you.
And somehow our faith was rekindled,
became stronger.

We learned to ask questions, to network with others.
Gentle hands showed us how
to hold you and feed you,
to take care of you.
We gave you your first bath
and saw your first haircut.

Your first Mother's Day, Father's Day, Thanksgiving:
We saw them come and go with other families.
You became known as (guess what?)
"Mayor of the NICU."
We had to find reasons
to laugh through our tears
We had to find small ways
to go through each day.

We learned to pick our fights,
said yes to some things
when there was no other way;
said "no" to some others,
and for that we are glad.

We loved you that first day.
We loved you through those nights.
We became the parents that God made us to be:
Mom and Dad to you,
who was born way too soon
but was loved from the start.

SOMETIMES GOD JUST KNOWS

God knows exactly
what you are thinking.
Not just sometimes—
but all the time.

In the church pew
during mass,
reflecting on last night's
troubling dream,
I remembered a long-ago funeral,
and the gospel of John:
"I am the Good Shepherd and know mine own."

I don't have to worry:
Jesus "got me" and I follow Him.
So I'm cool. So I'm fine.
So I should not be afraid.

As I silently talked to God,
the pianist played the first notes
of the Communion song:
David Haas. You Are Mine.
Do not be afraid, I am with you.
Coincidence? "God-incidence"?
I became amazed, humbled
by God's awesomeness!

God sent me a message,
talked back to me through music.

When the choir sang, the words turned
into a direct answer to my prayer:
I will come to you in the silence
I will lift you from all your fears.
The God I believe in is
a God of Love,
a God of Peace.
He is not racist, selfish, extreme.
He doesn't hate immigrants,
other languages, other countries.

We can't adjust our idea of "God"
to our own value systems,
refer to the Bible
to justify our self-centered,
divisive or hateful ways.

God doesn't condone violence or hate.
And while I do believe that
He wants me to be happy,
I can't imagine that He would approve
my being happy at others' expenses.

But how do Christians show resilience
with life's tribulations?

God gives hope. God gives strength.

THE LIGHTER SIDE OF THINGS

Of course I do enjoy
the lighter side of things.
I love life and enjoy
what it has to offer.
So many think
that I should instead
crawl under a rock
and hide there forever.

Running away from life
and hiding from myself,
hiding from my life
and what it may offer?
That's not who I am.

I love the life I have.
I'd rather have that life
than have nothing at all.
It is quite a challenge
to live my life as me,
but I can't just stand there
and watch it pass me by.
I make the best of things.
I embrace life fully,
let feelings flow freely,
through my heart and my soul.

Life is a gift from God,
and my cross: mine to bear.
I'm not ashamed of tears.

I'm not afraid of them.
I take them as they come,
then dry them and move on.
Pain may reside inside
but joy is in there, too.

In all the little things
that I find beautiful:
The sunshine, the sea,
nature's majesty,
Haiti, my birthplace,
people's sincerity.

I really like dancing,
love music even more,
can lose myself in books
and dream of writing them.
There's so much that I love
about life itself:
the flowers and the trees,
the cultural diversity
of the world around me.

And that's just about
the lighter side of things.
'Cause of course there's the love
I carry in my heart
for those people who are
so very dear to me.

So, no, I will not simply crawl
under a rock and hide,
when I'm grateful that God
made me the way I am:

Sunshine on Stormy Seas

with my head full of words
and my heart full of love,
eyes looking and finding
the good that life offers.

I know the bad is there,
crouched in some dark corner,
lurking its ugly head:
it's a reality.
It may hit hard at times,
punch me below the belt,
but still I find a way
to smile at life somehow.

I'm no perfect angel.
I just like living life
the way it is today.
I don't like to worry
about the past so much
for it is done and gone,
and now it's history.
And since I am not privy
to what the future holds
I'm content to exist
and to live my life now.

I WISH YOU WOULD

I wish You would give us a sign
that You are here, that You exist.
I wish You would give us a glimpse
of the Heavens, the After-life.
I wish You would send a signal,
a guarantee, a certainty
that all of this is not for naught
that there is still better to come.
I wish You would not be so tough
with all these wars, these fights, these deaths,
these disasters, these divisions,
all the things that we're going through.
I wish You would show us clearly
the light at the end of it all.
When we're going through the tunnel,
I wish You would show us the sky.
I wish You would show up one day
and let us know that it is You,
even if it's just for a day:
I wish You would do that indeed.
I wish You would let us feel You,
let us Hear You strongly, clearly,
so that our faith could be strengthened.

I wish You would not ask instead
that we believe only by faith,
for we face such tribulations.

We do believe
that You are real, that You exist.

71// Sunshine on Stormy Seas

I know not all agree it's true
but my plea is for those who do.
I wish You would take it easy
on all of us, give us a break.

I wish You would.
I know You could.
I wish You would.

LONG OVERDUE

Forty years of praying to God
when I am hurt.
Forty years of Him
never letting me down.

Forty years of facing danger,
of navigating life's troubled waters.
Forty years of Him
making sure I am safe,
keeping me from drowning.

Forty years of making mistakes,
of trying new things and doing wrong,
of losing my way,
of searching for answers and turning away.
Forty years of Him forgiving me,
being patient with me.

Forty Years of knowing temptation,
of falling down
and wanting to stay down.
Forty years of getting back up
because He carries me,
because He guides me.

Forty years of fear and doubt,
of trauma and loss,
of calling for Him in times of need.
Forty years of confronting my fears
because He is with me,
showing me that He is real.

Sunshine on Stormy Seas

Forty years of hope and comfort,
of angels sent my way.

Forty years of negligence,
indifference and selfishness,
of pushing Him away in anger.
Forty years of Him
loving me just the same,
taking me back with open arms.

Forty years of wondering
how I can make it every day.
Forty years of Him
making sure that I do.

Because of Him,
I am stronger today than I was yesterday,
I accept and understand more today
than I did yesterday,
I embrace Him more today
than I did yesterday.

He's always been the force
that keeps me on my feet
and makes me move forward.

When I was scared, angry, hurt,
and did not know the why's or how's,
when I did not have the answers,
when I wanted Him Gone,

God reached out, spoke to my heart.
He held me through the dark
until I felt better.

He would not let me
close my ears and my heart,
and push Him out of my life
as I asked naive questions:
"Why cannot I see you?"
"Why won't you send a sign?"

He sent me messengers
who spoke of Him
in ways that moved me.
Not magicians—people,
like you and me.

I remember it all.
I remember it well.
Forty years…

He has always been there.

And for that I thank Him.

JUST ENOUGH

God gives us just enough
    Enough courage to face the winds
    Enough courage to withstand the storm
    Enough courage to speak the truth
    Enough courage to take a stand

God gives us just enough
    Enough wisdom to understand
    Enough wisdom to make a choice
    Enough wisdom to tell a wrong
    Enough wisdom to let it go

God gives us just enough
    Enough heart to conquer fear
    Enough heart to fight for love
    Enough heart to help others
    Enough heart to lend a hand

God gives us just enough
    Enough light to drive out dark
    Enough light to chase the clouds
    Enough light to absorb pain
    Enough light to transform grief

God gives us just enough
    Enough tears to shed for loss
    Enough tears to wash away hurts
    Enough tears to say goodbye
    Enough tears to welcome good

God gives us just enough
> Enough laughter to swallow screams
> Enough laughter to lift spirits
> Enough laughter to savor life
> Enough laughter to spread out cheers

God gives us just enough
> Enough smiles to soothe others
> Enough smiles to appease ills
> Enough smiles to mend friendships
> Enough smiles to make new ones

God gives us just enough
> Enough joy to fill our souls
> Enough joy to breathe in life
> Enough joy to seize the day
> Enough joy to celebrate

God gives us just enough
> Enough strength to bear our crosses
> Enough strength to climb mountains
> Enough strength to walk our paths
> Enough strength to carry on

God gives us just enough
> Enough faith to lift us up
> Enough faith to pull us through
> Enough faith to sustain us
> Enough faith to feel His Grace

God gives us just enough.

ÂME MEURTRIE

Dans une église, l'heure était venue
de prier—pour qui ?
de prier pour moi,
de prier pour d'autres?

Comment choisir une requête
quand tout importe
dans ce monde à l'envers?
Ces enfants qui meurent de faim
en Afrique, et partout…
Et puis, les malheurs d'un séisme
qui a endeuillé les familles d'Haïti,
les a jetées à la rue…

Ame meurtrie, âme blessée,
âme meurtrie qui absorbe tout…

Et ces crimes affreux et insensés,
inexplicables et inexpliqués?
Ces actes cruels, inconcevables ?
Ces guerres qu'on veut justifier
et, pour ce, le nom de Dieu invoquer ?
Mais Notre Père n'a pas dit de tuer.

Ame meurtrie, âme blessée,
âme pour qui tout est cauchemar…

Et que dire de l'intolérance
qui existe pour la différence?
On veut tuer, éliminer,
pour cause de couleur ou d'ethnicité.

On veut bafouer, veut lapider.
On veut parler d'infériorité
pour masquer l'insécurité.

Ame meurtrie, âme indignée
âme impuissante et accablée…

Les requêtes sont nombreuses
Peut-être ne devrais-je prier
que pour moi ?
pour mon cœur qui soupire ?
Car quel grain de sable
remue un océan ?

Ame meurtrie, âme blessée,
âme qui voudrait tellement aider…

Je me tourne vers Dieu,
Lui qui voit ce que je ne vois pas,
Lui qui comprend ce que je ne comprends pas

Ame blessée, réconfortée,
âme meurtrie pétrie de foi…

IN SPITE OF IT ALL

They ask: How can you sing?
    How can you look so happy?
    How can you laugh?
    How can you even dance?

They say: How can you smile?
    Where do you find the courage?
    How can you have so much joy?

If you really want to know,
    here it is, I'll tell you how:
        I sing,
            not because I don't have
            a care in the world.
        I sing,
            despite all
            I have to care about.
        I dance,
            not because I don't feel
            weary and drained.
        I dance,
            despite feeling weary and
                      drained.
        And I talk and I laugh,
            despite my fears.
        I smile,
            despite my sorrows.

And I do it all
    Because of Faith.

God has given me
  the grace of Faith.
He has given me
  the gift of Faith.

I'm not so sure
  I can explain…
I just know
  that there's something.
    Something I look to
      when I feel lost.
    Something I cry to
      when I'm in pain.
    Something I hold on to
      when I panic.
    A belief
      that He is there.
    A belief
      that He listens.
    A belief
      that He loves me
    A belief
      that He won't fail me.

I don't really
  understand it.
I just let it
  stay there inside:
    In my heart
    and in my soul
      and it carries me
      through it all.

81// Sunshine on Stormy Seas

So I can sing
    because of it.
I can dance
    because it's there.
It strengthens me
    and gives me joy.
And so I laugh,
    in spite of tears,
        and I smile
            throughout my fears.
I love that God
    gave it to me,
        that something
            I don't really get,
        Something
            that I keep inside.

A ZEST FOR LIVING

I'm feeling this love for living
this love for living
right now
right about now
I got music
music in my head
I got music
music through my veins
pulsating to the rhythm
to the rhythm of my heart
and I just feel
I just feel so alive!
I just feel so
alive
I just
feel
so alive.

NO TIME

no time to write no time to dance no time to sit no time to talk no time to sleep no time to think no time to cry no time to sigh no time to scream no time to watch no time to fret no time to breathe no time to listen to my heart   just time to blend just time to work just time to file papers in that pile   no time to laugh no time to snap no time to cringe or to howl no time to do anything new no time to try anything else no time to paint or type or draw no time to read no time to bleed no time to come up for some air no time to wallow in these tears no time to relax with a beer   just time for a quick chat and a catch-up just time to see if I can keep up with it all

no time to go in for a play no time to go just for a day no time for leisure walks and window shopping strolls no time for heart-to-hearts or real conversations no time to wipe away the tears no time to squeeze the hand so near no time to sit up and reflect no time to stop and really think no time to eat no time for fancy cooking shows no time to try out new baked dough   just time for plain ole sustenance just time to make sure it gets all done   no time to be no time to see no time to feel   just time to grab just time to throw on a cover or a blanket or a sweater   just time to go

I HATE YOU

Gosh! How I hate you:
the thought of you,
the memory of you.
I hate that you ever happened.
I hate that things like you exist
to destroy and take lives
wherever you go.

You've been in the news a lot lately,
and whenever I see you,
disaster comes, too.
I hate mentioning you.
I hate the very sound of your name.

You've robbed me of so much:
my childhood, my dreams,
my home, my friends, my hopes
for the future of what was meant to be—
a world record,
the worst we've ever known.

You left my homeland on its knees,
hopeless, wounded, bleeding,
raw, exposed.
And you may not be done.
And you may well return

85// Sunshine on Stormy Seas

whenever you see fit.

What else is there to take?
What is it that you want?
Wasn't this performance
the one that stole the show,
the one that forced the world
to stop dead in its tracks?

All because of you,
so much is no longer!
You have blown away walls,
flattened roofs and bodies,
and turned into graveyards
places that once were safe.

After such awesome work,
I thought you'd be somewhere
quietly rejoicing
over what you have done.

I hate that you swallowed up
close to half a million souls.

I. hate. you!
I really, really do.

J'EN AI MARRE

C'est toujours la même histoire,
toujours le même scenario.
Haïti n'en finit pas:
manifestations, démonstrations,
émotions à fleur de peau.
J'en ai marre de la politique
et de ses politiciens.
MARRE!!!!
J'en ai ras le bol
de tous ceux qui ont soif
de pouvoir et d'argent.
Des morts inutiles
(*Poukisa gen moun
ki oblije pèdi lavi yo?*),
des affrontements entre
manifestants et police nationale.
Pourquoi? *Epi anyen menm.*
Ambitions politiques,
oubli de promesses
à un peuple désespéré.
*Tout moun ki pa nan politik
se lavi yo yap chèche.*
Ceux qui peuvent
font un peu plus,
ceux qui ont moins se battent
chaque jour
pour survivre.
Commerçants, petits marchands,
artisans, ouvriers : Ils vivent tous
au jour le jour, luttant pour
s'acheter un morceau de pain.

Enfants sans parents,
depuis le désastre
du 12 Janvier.
Hommes
qui ne se découragent pas,
femmes
qui se réveillent
chaque matin
et essaient
tant bien que mal
de continuer
à exister
dans cette atmosphère
volatile :
stoïquement, bravement.
Pères et mères de familles, étudiants,
grands-parents :
réalité impossible.
Y'en a marre. *Nou bouke!*

La plus belle preuve
de courage:
Avoir marre d'une situation
mais l'affronter
quand même
quotidiennement.
Haïti : petit pays.
Haïtiens : peuple courageux,
peuple valeureux.
Yo pa janm sispann batay!
Malgré tout.
En dépit de tout.

Armés d'un esprit combatif,
ils font face à la vie
et gardent l'espoir
d'un changement possible,
d'un lendemain meilleur.

Alors ils vont voter,
se laissent prendre
aux beaux discours
de ces messieurs et de ces dames
et disent avec leurs votes
qu'ils en ont marre aussi.
Impatients, fatigués,
ils prennent les rues,
armés de ce qu'ils trouvent,
et se laissent emporter
par la colère et le dégout.
Et l'émotion prend le dessus.

Bien sûr, il y en a, sans scrupules,
qui se mêlent à la foule,
en profitent pour piller,
voler et détruire,
et la manifestation
devient quelque chose
de bien plus menaçant.

J'en ai marre.

Le pays a déjà trop perdu
pour voir disparaitre
le peu qui lui reste.

Je suis fatiguée
de voir défiler
les mêmes images d'un film
que j'ai vu
trop de fois déjà.
La mise en scène et les acteurs
sont différents, peut-être,
et un nouveau directeur dirige l'acte,
mais c'est la même histoire.
remaniée quelque part,
légèrement modifiée
et j'en ai absolument marre!

J'en ai assez
de voir le pays où je suis née
s'enfoncer
de plus en plus
dans un trou
qui ne fait que s'agrandir
avec le temps!
J'en ai marre
de l'instabilité,
de l'indifférence,
des kidnappings et des épidémies.
J'en ai marre
des désastres naturels,
marre
des tragédies humaines.

Kilè nap ouvri je nou
poun manyen konprann
kisa ki nan enterè pa nou?

Kilè nap eseye kontwole emosyon nou
pou nou sèvi ak tèt nou
poun regle zafè nou?

BONHEUR DE PETITE FILLE

Je me réveille, matinale comme toujours.
Une petite toilette et je descends en courant.
Les pieds nus, je déplace le crochet et,
doucement, je me faufile par la porte de derrière.
Souriant au vent, je cours vers l'amandier.
Il est encore très tôt. L'impasse est presque vide;
le quartier dort encore et il fait un peu frais
grâce à la rosée sur les herbes,
sur les feuilles et les pétales des fleurs.
J'arrive sous l'amandier et, bonheur de petite fille,
il y a pleins d'amandes.
J'en prends à pleines mains.
J'en mange, en mets dans ma robe.
"Didine!" Le son d'une voix me parvient.
Quelqu'un s'est aperçu de ma petite escapade.
C'est ma grand-mère, Manman Etienne.
Elle appelle, je répond.
Il est temps d'arrêter et, de toute façon,
il commence à faire chaud et ma robe déborde.
Ravie, je file, heureuse et légère.
J'atteins la porte et rentre chez moi.
Que vais-je faire de toutes ces amandes?
Les manger, bien sûr,
et ensuite les casser
pour déguster le "nan nan" tout au fond.
Bonheur de petite fille.

JE N'OUBLIERAI JAMAIS

Je n'oublierai jamais
    l'année de ma philo
    l'année de l'insouciance
        avant l'incertitude

Je n'oublierai jamais
    les amis de l'école
    les copains du quartier
        et le temps des romances

Je n'oublierai jamais
    ce bal de fin d'année
    où j'ai tellement dansé
        j'en avais mal aux pieds

Je n'oublierai jamais
    les confidences sacrées
        partagées entre amis
        gardées dans le secret

Je n'oublierai jamais
    l'émotion d'un baiser volé
        au cours d'une danse
        ou dans une salle de ciné

Je n'oublierai jamais
    mon intrépidité
        quand avec l'uniforme
        j'ai fait de la moto

93// Sunshine on Stormy Seas

Je n'oublierai jamais
    le visage de mon père
    quand il m'a reconnu
        j'ai cru mourir de peur

Je n'oublierai jamais
    tous les rires aux éclats
    causés par de bonne blagues
    ou peut-être une farce

Je n'oublierai jamais
    l'effronterie de certains
    qui voulaient a tout prix
    choquer leur professeur

Je n'oublierai jamais
    ce que c'est d'être bleu
    dans une faculté
    où je m'étais inscrite

        Mi-figue, mi-raisin
        je subissais mon sort
        et maintenant ce temps-là
        je me le rappelle bien

Je n'oublierai jamais
    quand à la file indienne
    on sortait en silence
    et la classe restait vide

Je n'oublierai jamais
    ces samedis où, hardies,
    on décidait de faire
    l'école buissonnière

Je n'oublierai jamais
      les regards échanges
      les mots à demi-dits
      et les fou-rires subits

Je n'oublierai jamais
      les refrains enchainants
      dont on ne se lassait pas
      malgré les punitions

Je n'oublierai jamais
      les moments spontanés
      où on faisait une ronde
      ou même un carnaval

Je n'oublierai jamais
      « Mais quelle impertinence ! »
      « Mesdemoiselles, calmez-vous! »
      C'était assez courant

Je n'oublierai jamais
      que malgré les temps sombres
      on trouvait le moyen
      de sourire à la vie

Je n'oublierai jamais
      qu'on avait peur, c'est vrai
      mais qu'on voulait quand même
      profiter de la vie

Je n'oublierai jamais
      qu'on se disait souvent
      « Deux jours à vivre, *tande !*
      Rès la pou anba tè »

Je n'oublierai jamais
        les souvenirs créés
        au cours de ces années
        où j'achevais mes classes

Je n'oublierai jamais
        la terre qui m'a offert
        de si beaux souvenirs
        de mon temps d'écolière

Insigne de mon enfance
de mon adolescence,
        Haïti de mon cœur,
              je n'oublierai jamais.

NOSTALGIE

Lorsque je vois ces cieux,
je pense à d'autres cieux,
d'autres nuages,
d'autres paysages.

Lorsque je vois ces plages,
je pense à d'autres plages,
d'autres vagues,
d'autres grains de sable.

Je me revois chez moi,
perdue dans mes rêveries,
le regard tourné
vers la lune suspendue.

De la cuisine parfois
je regarde des arbres
et là encore je vois
d'autres arbres, d'autres feuillages.

Je partage mes souvenirs
avec qui veut l'entendre:
« Cette vue me rappelle
celle que j'avais de ma chambre.
Je pouvais voir les arbres de la fenêtre aussi. »

Milles petits « rien du tout »
me ramènent en arrière,
me forcent à reconnaître
cette mélancolie.

Elle me laisse perplexe, cette nostalgie cachée,
puisque tout a changé;
rien n'est plus comme avant.

Et pourtant elle est là,
assourdie, mais constante.
Elle me prend par la gorge,
parfois me serre le ventre.

Le cœur et le cerveau
refusent d'oublier.

Moi je suis bien ici.
Je me suis bien adaptée
mais je ne peux empêcher
ce que fait ma mémoire.

Elle me joue de petits tours,
me ramène au passé,
me surprend toujours
par son intensité.

Et donc on joue ce jeu
où j'embrasse le présent,
complètement, totalement,
sans aucune réserve.

Et elle, elle prend le temps
de réveiller en moi
des souvenirs endormis
et des sons oubliés.

BONJOUR, SOLEIL!

Bonjour, Soleil !
Tu t'es levé comme chaque matin.
Je pense à Haïti, Soleil.
Donne-moi des nouvelles du pays.
Qui se réveille en ce moment ?
Dans la maison où j'ai grandi,
qui est déjà sur pied ?
Lorsque tu perces à peine le ciel,
il y a sûrement, quelque part,
certains qui boivent un p'tit café,
qui mangent un petit morceau de pain
car ils t'ont vu te réveiller.
Et la marchande de riz ?
Est-elle déjà en route vers le marché ?
Dis-moi donc, Soleil,
éclaires-tu ses pas sur la route, Soleil ?
Et celle qui est toujours au coin,
tout près de l'hôtel, tous les matins ?
L'as-tu réveillée, elle aussi,
ou bien est-elle encore endormie ?
Ton reflet a-t-il à cette heure pénétré
les rideaux des fenêtres ?
Les enfants s'apprêtent-ils
pour l'école maintenant ?
Soleil, que révèlent tes rayons ?
Que voient les passants matinaux ?
Qu'exposent les premières heures
lorsque l'ombre devient lumière
et la nuit redevient jour ?
Serait-ce encore une tragédie, Soleil ?
Un meurtre ? Un kidnapping ?

99// Sunshine on Stormy Seas

Soleil, toi, tu ne caches rien.
Avec toi, tout est dénudé.
Ta présence sonne l'alarme,
dévoile l'horreur de la nuit.
Soleil, j'aime bien que tu sois là, oui,
que tu brilles quand même sur Haïti.
Quand tu te montres tous les matins,
une énergie s'éveille et se propage.
Haïti vit. Elle existe.
Dieu savait bien ce qu'Il faisait
lorsqu'Il t'a fait briller, Soleil.
Te rends-tu compte
combien tu comptes
pour ceux qui vivent en Haïti ?

MEMORIES

In the playground,
we stood in circles—
School days
School friends
Jokes and laughter
Feuds and confrontations
Gossips

Feelings—hurt
Stares—cutting
Brains—working
    Refuting arguments

We sat in classrooms
    listened to teachers
    discussed literature
    debated philosophy
        —serious faced, naïve,
        unaware of the dangers
        of the dark corners
            in a country already in turmoil
            with zenglendos

Haitian abroad! I left for college.
    graduated
    missed home
    returned
        every chance I got
            —summer breaks, holidays

Sunshine on Stormy Seas

I could not stay away
>even though the news streamed in:
>>a friend was kidnapped,
>>a friend's dad, then a friend of a friend.
>>>What if, what if?
>>>Nothing could hide me
>>>from my thoughts.
>>>>"No one is truly safe."

Then—
>a husband, a brother, a wife.
>a brother, a sister, a cousin.
>>Some never returned.
>>>How much I prayed for them
>>>to God, my superman

Still I went back,
>my heart—a hammer
>I didn't leave the house.
>>—serious faced, but no longer naïve,
>>aware of the dangers
>>of the dark corners
>>>in a country in turmoil

"He's the only mother he's got."
>Yet, my heart yearned
>>for the streets,
>>to taste what I once knew,
>>to appreciate what still is.
>>>So many memories
>>>So many firsts
>>>>I could never forget.

Haiti.
> This land a speck in the world—
> but its roots dig deep into my heart.

I cannot forget.
I want to go back.

LA CAMÉRA

Elle raconte tant d'histoires. Saisit le moment sur le vif, le capture, l'immortalise. Elle recèle tant de fonctions: elle amuse, justifie, prouve, informe et contredit. Ses photos agitent la conscience, provoquent le sourire, l'étonnement, la consternation! La caméra, d'elle même, se dirige vers les acteurs—certains choisis, d'autres inédits—et les invite à jouer un rôle. (Quel théâtre ! Attention, paparazzis !) Sans elle, que regarderions-nous vraiment en tournant les pages des revues, des magazines? C'est à se demander ce que faisaient les gens avant qu'elle ne devienne célèbre. La caméra, c'est comme un lit : nécessaire, indispensable. Comme le téléphone ou la télé. On ne s'imagine plus aller nulle part sans s'assurer qu'elle est bien là ; come une montre, un portefeuille ou un permis. Amusante notre obsession (notre compulsion !) à l'utiliser. Elle change les choses, réclame sa place, chaque jour, chaque seconde. Je la critique. Je l'admire. Qu'elle serait moche, la vie, sans les photos de la camera.

REGRETS

I should have known better,
should have stayed the course.
Instead I chose shorter, faster and easier.
I should have thought harder,
should have acted smarter.
Instead I changed my mind, became prim and proper.
I should have been wiser and should have aimed higher.
Instead I decided to settle for safer.
I should have been bolder, less fearful and braver.
Instead I chose to do I what I thought was nicer.
I should have been patient
and should have stayed longer.
Instead I chose the path that just seemed much simpler.
I should have remembered that my dreams were bigger.
Instead I was restless and opted for quicker.
I should have decided to go a lot further.
Instead, I rushed towards what I thought was brighter.
I should have remembered better late than never.
Instead I turned away from what was much greater.

CHÉRI, DOUDOU, AMOUR

Chéri, doudou, amour,
laisse-moi tranquille, veux-tu ?
Il y a bien trop longtemps
que tu joues à ce jeu.

Chéri, doudou, amour,
j'ai vraiment essayé
d'avoir une autre approche.
Me suis dit que, peut-être,
mon instinct me trompait.

Chéri, doudou, amour,
quelle perte ça a été
de vouloir te donner
le bénéfice du doute—
de croire que tu étais
devenu un peu plus mûr.

Tu es resté, bien sûr,
comme tu l'étais toujours.
Il paraît, après tout,
que certaines choses demeurent.

Chéri, doudou, amour,
c'était quoi, après tout,
le but de cette comédie ?
Qui cherchais-tu à plaire ?
Que cherchais tu à faire ?

Chéri, doudou, amour,
penses-tu vraiment savoir
ce qui est important ?
Crois-tu vraiment comprendre
pourquoi, toi, tu existes ?

Chéri, doudou, amour,
il est temps de cesser
ces petits jeux ridicules.
Regarde autour de toi.
Tout le monde a grandi.

Chéri, doudou, amour,
laisse-moi tranquille, veux-tu ?
J'ai vraiment plus envie.
Le jeu a trop duré.

Chéri, doudou, amour,
fais ce que tu as à faire.
Ne le fais pour personne.
Fais-le surtout pour toi.

Chéri, doudou, amour,
Je ne voulais pas te dire
qu'au fond je m'attendais
à toutes sortes d'inepties.
Te connaissant si bien,
j'ai prédit le délire.

Chéri, doudou, amour,
rien ne m'étonne vraiment.
On n'est plus sûr de rien,
sauf peut-être de soi-même.

Chéri, doudou, amour,
Je savais qu'tôt ou tard
ça se passerait ainsi.
Que tu ne pourrais prétendre
ce que tu ne comprends pas.

Chéri, doudou, amour,
je n'aime pas m'accrocher
aux idées du passé.
Je ne suis pas parfaite.
J'ai commis mes erreurs.

Chéri, doudou, amour,
tu ne les reconnais pas,
les erreurs de ton art ?
J'aurais dû, avant toi,
te les montrer du doigt.

Chéri, doudou, amour,
j'aurais dû simplement
écouter ma conscience
qui me disait clairement
de dire non tout bonnement.

Chéri, doudou, amour,
parfois c'est mieux de laisser
les choses comme elles sont.
Tu es bien où tu es ;
tu aimes ce que tu es.
Je suis bien dans mon coin,
et j'aime bien qui je suis.

BECAUSE I LOVE YOU & MISS YOU SO

Because I love you,
I miss you now that you are gone,
and because I love you,
I keep your memory alive.

Because I love you
and want to remember you,
on Good Fridays, I bring home fish,
and cabbage, and olive oil.

Because I love you,
I cook a special meal on Christmas Day,
and garnish the table
with the traditional dishes of your table.
I spice up my food just like you did.

Because I love you and miss you so,
Every New Year's Eve, I say a prayer
and your face flashes in my mind.
I remember the special blessing
you gave at midnight.
Couldn't go out to dance until you did.

Because I love you but can't see you,
I think of your words and use them a lot.
I sing the songs you used to sing,
recite the poems you read to me.

Because I love you
and don't want to forget you,
I use the manners I learned from you,
the expressions I heard you use.
I care for my plants, just for you,
and I wish my thumbs
were as good as yours were.

Because I love you and remember you,
I try to act the way you taught me,
to remember the poor
the way you used to.
I carry your teachings
in my everyday life.
I am not as good as you,
but I'm still learning.

Because I love you,
I remember names
I should have forgotten,
I remember those
who knew me as a child.

Because I love you and miss you so,
I hope one day to see you again,
and I hope you'll say
that I make you proud
that you see a little bit of who you were
in who I've become.

THANK YOU

For all the times that you believed
when I started doubting myself.
For all the kind words that you spoke
when I was feeling dejected.
For the support, for being there.
For the prayers and for your faith.

For the moments you shared with me.
and for choosing to be there for me.
For listening and for caring,
for looking up when I looked down.
For the encouragement, the praise,
for the laughter and for the tears.
For holding hands and for the push.
For seeing good when I saw bad.
For yelling out, "Keep holding on."
and whispering that God is good.
For sending text messages and for calling.
For being patient when I snapped.
For never letting me give up,
and not cutting me any slack.
For pulling me up off the ground
and comforting me when I cried.
For joining your voices to mine
and understanding my mood swings.
For never offering pity,
and for never looking down on me.
For choosing to tell me the truth.
For standing by without a word.
For looking past appearances,
for teaching me about Faith.

111// Sunshine on Stormy Seas

For accepting me as I am
and for just trying to understand.
For finding resources and help,
for providing hugs and kisses.
For being the reason I smile
and throwing your glove in the fight.
For not letting me lose myself
and staying on the road with me.
For the nights out and for the fun,
for cracking jokes and for singing.
For taking time to say hello
and meeting me half-way on those days.
For respecting my life, my choice,
and not treating me differently.
For showing me that you care.
For all the little ways you are there.
For the strength that comes from your love:

Thank You.

YOU HAVE TO STAY

Who will be my friend,
my partner, my soul-mate,
if you don't?

You have to stay.

Who will cheer me on,
with a hug and a kiss,
if you don't?

You have to stay.

Who will care for me,
fight for me, and with me
if you don't?

You have to stay.

Who will help me out,
support me, protect me
if you don't?

You have to stay.

Who will make me think,
make me wait, make me try,
if you don't?

You have to stay.

Sunshine on Stormy Seas

Who will take the time
that it takes to know me
if you don't?

You have to stay.

Who will walk with me,
hope with me,
dream with me,
if you don't?

You have to stay.

Who will understand,
hold my hand, dry my tears
if you don't?

You have to stay.

Who will share my joys,
feel my pain, see my fears
if you don't?

You have to stay.

Who will look at me,
make me laugh,
make me smile
if you don't?

YOU HAVE TO STAY.

WHAT A GUY!

He's not just any guy.

He's the guy who works hard,
he's the guy who prays hard.
He's the guy who gets it,
the guy who understands.

A serious kind of guy
Not always, just enough.

A guy who keeps it real,
a guy who doesn't run.
He's the guy who holds you
when your tears are falling.
He's the guy who helps you
when you're not doing well.

He's really a good guy,
he's a good guy indeed.

The guy who lends a hand
whenever, wherever.
The guy who'll lift you up
when you fall on your knees.

What a guy, what a friend!
What a good-hearted man.

Doesn't talk all that much,
could be described as shy,
though sometimes he lets go
and says quite a mouthful.

Light-hearted or moody,
he's quite the guy for sure.

He's the guy who listens,
the guy who tries new things.
He's the guy who will laugh
when it is least expected.
Focused and determined
in his goals and his dreams,
keeps his eyes on the prize,
keeps hitting at the ball.

He wants to leave his mark.
He is well on his way.

Today he turns forty;
he looks like he's thirty.
He's done quite well so far:
more than was predicted,
better than expected,
from hot-headed young boy
to clear-headed strong man.

He is forty years young,
he is forty years strong.

He's not just any guy.
He's really quite a guy.

THE STORY OF US

I still remember how I felt
the day that you and I first met,
when you decided that my pen
was yours to keep and that was that.
I still remember how I felt
when we went out on our first date.
When your car broke down on the road
and I decided I would help.
I still remember it all:
our college years,
our dating years,
our times dancing and partying.
Our quiet times, our busy times
in the library studying,
talking and getting to know you.
Our happy times, our fun times
at the movies or the diner.
I remember us together,
huddled side by side on the stairs,
our heads touching while you helped me
fill out the forms you had brought me.
You'd identified scholarships
for which you thought I should apply.
I had my doubts, even refused
but you pressed on, believed in me.
Right outside of the main lobby
of the college where we first met,
you stayed by my side and made sure
I completed them correctly.
I remember us hanging out
watching TV, watching a game.

I remember our private times,
our romance and all our struggles.
I remember our hard times, too,
when the future became the now,
when things started getting serious.
Graduating and then working.
Suddenly it was time to ask:
Are we looking at the future?
Do we move in, who's moving where?
I remember all the questions,
the decisions we had to make.
So many talks and discussions,
so many doubts, hesitation.
I remember our engagement
after that party at my house.
How you simply showed me that ring
how I could only stare at it.
I really didn't understand.
It really didn't dawn on me
that you were proposing to me.
For a minute I was speechless,
my mind went blank and my thoughts froze.
I wonder if you remember…
It was my birthday, remember?
I remember the excitement,
the joy, the fear, the challenges.
I remember planning our day
to make it just what we wanted.
Of course we fought over the list
(we're both so opinionated.)
But we gave in when it mattered;
you supported the big choices
and in the end, we were happy
(It really was a special day.)

Some things are still the same, you know:
the way I feel when you are near,
the emptiness when you're not here,
the despair brought on by the fear
of thinking of life without you.
I love you so, you just don't know.
It doesn't even feel as if
we've been at it for all these years.
We share a life, we have a son,
we've faced some pretty crazy things.
So, yes, I know that time has passed,
but it really doesn't matter.
In my mind's eye, I see it all
as if it was just yesterday:
our story, the good and the bad,
how we came to be you and me.
Thinking back to old hurts I've had,
now I see how they weren't real.
But though they were tough to go through
I'm grateful for all that I've learned,
for when you came along I knew,
I just knew it wasn't the same.
In some ways we're so different:
me with my art, you with your sports,
me daydreaming and you planning.
The extrovert, the introvert,
the sensitive, the practical,
both independent to a fault.
But we're so happy when we laugh,
when we dance to our favorite songs.
Life feels fuller, richer, better,
more complete and just right with you.
The story of us is all this.
A sweet, sweet song deep in my heart.

REGULAR GUY

He's a regular guy.
He likes sports,
likes to sleep,
is a hearty eater.

He's a regular guy.
He enjoys a good time
as much as the next dude;
he tells jokes then he laughs,
he can be quite funny.
He wakes up every day
and gets ready for work,
complaining all the while
because he's still sleepy.

He's a regular guy.
He's not for the spotlight.
Flies under the radar.
Prefers to keep quiet
unless he knows you well.

He's a regular guy.
He's handsome and he's smart.
He's carefree but serious.
He handles challenges
as well as he knows how.

He's a regular guy.
Loves lazy summer days,
barbecues and parties,
swimming in the ocean
or diving in the pool.
He's a regular guy.
Dinner and a movie,
Party and some music.
He's quite good at dancing.
In fact he's like a pro.

He's jut a special guy:
A kind-hearted rough boy
who goes on about life
with courage and with strength.
He's a special father
who loves that little boy
who looks so much like him.
In fact he's a rare find,
precious stone in the raw,
not polished to the max
but he stands above most.

He's as real as they get.
Will try with all his heart.
So cute when he does that.
Endearing with flowers,
charming when bearing gifts.
He can be sweet as pie!
He's full of life, you know:
a go-getter of sorts.
Respects the traditions.

Understands.

FORTY

Forty is awesome!
Forty is great!
Forty is just right!
Forty's cool.
It's forty years of being you
And what a great **YOU** you have been!
You've tried new things, and done good deeds,
suffered defeats, earned victories.
It took forty years to create
the you who's standing here today:
a good-looking and sexy man,
a stylish woman, full of bold moves.
Someone who'd rather walk the walk.
Someone who won't just talk the talk.
It's forty years to learn and grow
And you certainly did just that!
It's forty years of being smart,
sensitive you—loving and fun.
It's forty years of living life,
of learning lessons, making gains.
Realizing mistakes you've made,
and getting up to try again.
It's forty years of forging dreams,
of thinking hard, of being bold.
It's forty years to thrive and know
what you will do and where you'll go.
Forty years allow confidence
From forty years of experience.
You know so much more than before.
You'll do so much more than before.

Create more ways to leave your mark
and put your own stamp on the world.
Cause you're forty and that's just it:
You're forty years stronger, forty years better.

www.ingramcontent.com/pod-product-compliance
Lightning Source LLC
Chambersburg PA
CBHW020942090426
42736CB00010B/1231